JEWISH CUISINE COOKBOOK

Oriental charm of gourmet dishes

by

HANS MEYER

ISBN: 9798741013885

Jewish cuisine

The cuisine of Israel is considered to be a part of the Mediterranean cuisine, so olive oil, vegetables, fruits, fish, legumes are common here. However, the Jewish cuisine has significant differences from the culinary traditions of the Mediterranean countries. First of all, because of Judaism and Arab influence, as well as the culture of the three largest sub-ethnic communities - Ashkenazi (Eastern European Jews), Sephardic (Spanish Jews) and Yemeni Jews. Let's talk about everything.

Judaism requires observance of the laws of kosher. All products are divided into kosher (permitted) and tref (prohibited). Kosher products, in turn, are divided into meat, dairy and parve (neutral). The joint use of meat and dairy products is strictly prohibited.

It is allowed to eat only the meat of herbivores and at the same time artiodactyls (cows, sheep, goats and others), and the slaughter of animals must take place strictly according to a ritual called shechita and exclusively by a specialist who has undergone a long training, passed the exam and received the right to perform shechita. Blood is also prohibited by kashrut, so the meat is soaked in water, sprinkled with coarse salt, and then washed to get rid of the blood.

Fish is considered to be kosher if it spawns and has scales, fins, gills, and a spine. Caviar can only be eaten from kosher fish. For example, sturgeon and beluga are non-kosher fish, so black caviar is trefl; red (salmon) caviar is allowed. Various molluscs and crustaceans are tref.

It is allowed to cook only domestic poultry: chickens, turkeys, ducks, geese. Eggs are edible only if they are from kosher birds.

Thus, a product derived from a non-kosher organism is also non-kosher. The only exception is honey, because by kosher it is considered to be a vegetable product.

During the celebration of Pesach (Easter), it is forbidden to eat or even keep fermented dough products (flour, malt, cereal) in the house.

On Saturdays, Jews observe Shabbat, so they eat dishes specially prepared on Friday. The traditional Saturday dish is cholent, which consists of meat, vegetables, beans and cereals. Cholent languishes in a pot from late Friday evening to Saturday. Challah (wicker bread) is also eaten on Shabbat.

It is worth noting that the laws of kosher may vary slightly in different Jewish communities.

All products are checked for kosher by a trained professional (mashgiah) or a rabbi.

The influence of Arab culture led to the emergence of hummus, falafel, shawarma, burek pies and other dishes in Israeli cuisine.

Finally, large Jewish communities have brought many famous dishes to Israeli cuisine. These are traditional Ashkenazi dishes: tsimes (vegetable stew), gefilte fish (stuffed fish), kugel (casserole), forshmak (herring appetizer), matsebray (matzo snack), bagel (bagel) and many others. The Sephardim made such a contribution: shakshuka (fried eggs in tomato sauce), couscous, mafrum (stuffed potatoes), hraime (spicy fish), sambusaki pies and others. Yemenite Jews traditionally prepared maluah (pancake puff pastry), jachnun (traditional Sabbath dish puff pastry), hawaij seasoning, sauce zhug.

The secrets of Jewish cuisine

The basis of the cuisine is fruits, fish and dairy products. And these are healthy food products. But at the same time, everything should be prepared and consumed according to the rules of kosher. For example, you cannot combine meat and dairy products. They must be cooked in different vessels; they must also be eaten separately.

In addition, you cannot mix meat with fish in the same dish. Combinations of milk and chicken (even in separate vessels), beef and fish, and other similar combinations should not be allowed in one meal. The kashrut rules are known enough, and it is rather problematic to list them all.

It is worth highlighting the main ones.

Products prohibited for Jews include:

- animal blood;
- pork;
- meat of predators, including birds of prey and fish;
- caviar of predatory fish;
- hare;
- fish without scales;
- bird eggs with blood clots (however, they can be removed).

Among the most common products for consumption are poultry, liver.

In addition, Jews include goose fat in their diet, choosing it over chicken fat.

Fish is a national food found in the daily diet, especially pike and tuna.

Also in the diet of Jews there are dairy and vegetable products. Among all the foods, Jews prefer stuffed ones.

The chefs have learned how to make them to perfection. They can make stuffed meat, poultry, fish, make hearty and mouth-watering rolls. Jews also love first courses, preferring broths and vegetable soups.

Separately, one can single out such a dish as kreplach, which resembles our dumplings with cheese filling or dried fruit filling.

Another striking feature of Jewish cuisine is the significant amount of flour products.

Most often, these are dough blanks, which can be stored for a long time, and then used for cooking pies and other dishes.

Also, national confectionery delicacies are distinguished, namely teiglach, lekah, challah. They are made from wheat flour with nuts, honey, poppy seeds and raisins.

Spices are indispensable components of meals. They are used with caution and in metered amounts. Jews are convinced that spices should complement the dish, not overpower its taste.

The most popular flour product is matzo. These are unleavened cakes made of flour and water that can be stored for a long time. They are used as bread, snacks are spread on them, for example, herring forshmak, muhammaru (walnut and baked pepper puree), hummus (pea paste with spices), they are used as cake cakes.

Jewish salads and snacks

Salads and snacks are not very common in Jewish cuisine. A significant place is occupied by forshmak (herring puree), as well as simply chopped herring. Jews love this delicious fish in all its forms, so a lot of recipes are known with it.

Among other types of snacks, eggs chopped with onions are distinguished (they are additionally fried in butter, vegetable oil or goose fat), radish with lard, and hehakte leber (plowed from the liver).

Salads are mostly very simple and affordable, for example: beetroot (boiled and chopped beets, grated horseradish, dressing with vegetable oil, vinegar, salt and sugar); potato (boiled and diced potatoes, chopped onions, pepper, salt, vinegar and mayonnaise dressing); cucumber and egg (fresh cucumbers, green onions, egg, salt and goose fat dressing).

First and second courses are the main diet. From the first courses, broths from poultry, veal and vegetable soups are common. Broths are often made with noodles, homemade croutons and flour dressings.

One of the common first courses is cold beetroot soup. All spices are used very carefully so as not to overpower the taste of the food.

Also in demand are such types of first courses as: cold sweet borsch with candied fruits and dried fruits; bean and potato soup; cold red borscht; pea soup with meat; potato soup with milk; milk soup with dumplings; barley soup.

Second courses are mostly presented with chopped rolls and stuffed dishes. Goose and chicken necks are very popular.

Many tourists are inclined to believe that this is more a ritual and a tribute to tradition than a really favorite dish. Indeed, the preparation of the poultry neck is quite intricate.

First you need to get the middle out of the bird's neck so as not to damage the skin, then the bones are removed, and the meat is crushed. After that, it is fried in goose fat along with flour and onions.

The next step is to put the food back into the neck and fry it until it has a characteristic golden brown crust.

Fish has a special place in Israeli cooking (it must have scales, fins and gills, only this is considered kosher). The Jews also love stuffed fish.

Fillings can be any, except for meat. The general name for all stuffed fish is gefilte fish.

Israeli restaurants even offer fish stuffed with other fish, which is considered to be a gourmet meal.

They also love this product in a pickled or grilled (musht) form.

In total, about 15 methods of marinating fish are known, especially tuna, which is very revered. Among the side dishes for the main courses, the following are held in high esteem: hummus (pea puree with garlic and onions); falafel (soy balls); tahini (ground onion-tomato-sesame mass).

By the way, the seasonings used differ in different regions of the country, so the dishes are different, and tourists can go on a real gastronomic journey.
You can not ignore such delicious dishes as: *Hraime.* This is any fish with scales that is baked with a spicy sauce. Lamb with couscous. It is usually baked and served with boiled porridge. Eggplant with chicken. In many ways, the food is similar to a stew.

Mafrum. These are potatoes, which the Jews skillfully stuff with minced meat. *Kugel.* It resembles both a casserole and a pudding at the same time. It contains rice-pasta-potato-beetroot mass.

Baking

Baking is presented in huge quantities: lekah, homentash, matzah, kneidlach, challah and many others.

A specific feature is that most dough products are blanks for other foods that can be stored for a long time. But one cannot but name individual flour dishes: *Khomentash*. These are hearty pies that are abundantly stuffed with poppy seeds. *Challah*. This is a special kind of bread - wicker bread. It also contains poppy seeds or sesame seeds. This dish is served on Saturday.

Kneidlach. These are hearty and small dumplings that are boiled in broth. Matzo. It is a thin and crunchy sheet made from dough (water and flour).

Matze Braye. The dish consists of soaked matzo sheets, which are subsequently fried in goose fat with eggs and onions. And the remaining crumbs are used to bake pancakes, which are called mace latkes.

Lackach. These are delicious almond-flavored gingerbread cookies.

Latkes. This is the name for Jewish potato pancakes, which housewives often cook at home.

Mandalas. These are carvings made of simple dough, which are rolled very thinly. The figurines are fried in boiling oil and served with the first courses.

Bagel. These are bagels made from dough, first boiled and then baked.

Sufganiet. Dessert is a donut filled with jelly or jam.

Khremzlakh. This is our familiar biscuit biscuit. Pancakes. This is the name for Jewish pancakes, in which any filling can be wrapped.

Jewish cuisine is multifaceted and varied, despite restrictions on the permitted products. Over the years, chefs have learned to use food products that are acceptable for kashrut so that the dishes delight in taste, appetizing and aroma. You can choose the recipe you like with step-by-step photos from the ones offered on this page and prepare a delicious meal.

Israeli cuisine continues to improve today, with new combinations of ingredients and special processing methods.

Stew of beef in onion sauce

Ingredients

beef pulp (from the breast, or from the shoulder, boneless only) - I have 1200 gr. (it is possible, even better, if there is more)
flour, a little less than a tablespoon of
vegetable oil, 2 tbsp.
onions -4 medium onions, cut into wide rings (1.25 cm wide)
garlic-4 pieces, peeled and finely chopped
tomato juice-250 ml.
salt
freshly ground black pepper
thyme
red pepper - 1/2 tsp
bay leaf - 1-2 pieces
carrots - 4 cut diagonally in 6 mm strips

Step by step cooking recipe

Rinse the meat under running water, dry thoroughly with paper towels

Dust the meat on all sides with flour

In a cauldron or in a deep frying pan, warm up 1 a tablespoon of vegetable oil (at medium temperature)

Fry the meat first on one side for 5-7 minutes, then turn over and fry on the other side for 5-7 minutes

Remove the meat from the pan onto a plate

Preheat the oven to 170 degrees

Add more to the pan a spoonful of oil

Fry the onion for 4-5 minutes

Add garlic to the onion and fry for a minute

Pour tomato juice, mix

Salt and pepper from the mill, add thyme, red pepper and bay leaf

Put the meat back in the pan (or a cauldron, it is much more convenient)

Add water so that the meat is covered almost to the very top

Bring to a boil

Seal the pan (cauldron) carefully cover and put in the oven for 3-3.5 hours, until the meat is softest (check with a fork)

Remove from the oven, add carrots to the sauce, close the lid again and simmer for another 30 minutes

Remove from the oven, remove the lid

Put the meat on a dish, Spread the onion-carrot sauce around the meat

You can garnish with parsley

Croquettes - according to the Baghdad Jews' recipe

Croquettes - oblong cutlets, which are fried in oil. The word itself is of French origin, however, the dish became popular outside of France, for example, the British liked it. And later, already as a "traditional English dish", it came to India. It was in India that this name was borrowed by the Jewish communities of Bombay and Calcutta - the Baghdad Jews. Croquettes began to be called cutlets, which, by the way, were not local, but were brought to India at the beginning of the 19th century by Jewish settlers from Iraq. This was not the end of the metamorphosis with the cutlets. In addition to the name, the dish also borrowed typical Indian spices. Jewish women living in India began to add ginger, turmeric and masala to traditional rice and garlic

Ingredients

round rice - 200 g
minced chicken - 400 g
garlic - 2-3 cloves
ginger root - 3 cm
Turmeric - 1 tsp
cilantro (without sticks) - 1 bunch
Salt - 2 pinches
olive oil for frying

Preparation

Boil rice. After boiling, keep the rice on the fire for 15 minutes, then drain the water.

Mix the minced chicken with the grated ginger and garlic.

Add turmeric, cilantro, salt, and then rice.

Make oblong cutlets from this mixture.

Fry them on all sides in vegetable / olive oil.

Babagunush

Babagunush is a very popular appetizer in oriental cuisine, especially in Lebanon and Israel. It is prepared from eggplants, which are pre-baked in the oven. An integral part of the dish is tahini - a sesame seed paste. In the East, as a rule, you can buy it in any supermarket. A simple recipe for making eggplant babaganush in Israeli style is described step by step below.

Ingredients

eggplant 5 pcs.
sesame paste (tahini) 5 tablespoons
garlic 1 clove
lemon juice 2 tablespoons
olive oil 4 tablespoons
edible salt to taste
dried basil 0.5 tsp

Preparation

Wash the eggplants, wipe off moisture.

Wrap each vegetable in foil and send to the oven.

Bake the eggplant at 200 degrees for about an hour.

When the allotted time has passed, remove the vegetables from the oven and separate the flesh from the skin.

After baking, it is very easy to do it even with a tablespoon.

Transfer the eggplant pulp to a bowl, add the garlic clove and blend with a hand blender.

Add sesame paste to the resulting mass and stir thoroughly.

Pour in lemon juice and olive oil, salt to taste and stir again.

Remove the eggplant babaganush in the refrigerator for 1-2 hours to infuse.

The consistency of the finished snack is puree like in the photo.

Drizzle over the babaganush with olive oil and sprinkle with dry basil before serving.

You can spread the snack on bread, or you can dip crispy pita bread in it.

Latkes

Latkes can also be made from unpeeled potatoes. The potato skins give the dish a mouth-watering brown color and a crispier crust. Just remember to wash the root crop thoroughly.

To make the dish tasty, you must adhere to some rules: since the potatoes darken quickly, they must be grated very quickly; squeeze the root crop thoroughly (wet potatoes make ordinary pancakes saturated with fat); fry potato cakes only in well-heated oil, otherwise you won't get a crispy crust.

Ingredients

Potatoes 6 pcs.
Bulb onion 1 pc.
Chicken eggs 2 pcs.
Wheat flour 1/2 cup
Edible salt to taste
Ground black pepper to taste
Vegetable oil as needed

Preparation

Peel the potatoes, wash and grate on a coarse grater.

Peel the onion, chop finely and add to the potatoes.

By the way, it is the onion that retains the color of the vegetable, and it does not darken so quickly.

Beat two eggs into a separate bowl and add a little flour.

Season with salt and pepper to taste.

Stir the resulting mixture until smooth.

Squeeze the grated potatoes well with your hands.

Do this as carefully as possible; the potatoes must be dry to form a crust.

Combine the squeezed vegetable with the egg and flour mixture. Mix thoroughly.

Place the skillet on the stove and pour the vegetable oil into it.

When the oil has warmed up well, spoon the minced potatoes and place them in the skillet.

Fry the latkes until crispy on both sides. When the tortillas are cooked, remove them from the pan and place them on a paper towel.

Do not stack only latkes one by one. This can cause them to become moist and lose their crispy texture.

Serve Jewish pancakes with sour cream or fresh vegetables. Although classic latkes are served with apple puree.

Forshmak classic

Forshmak is a dish of Jewish cuisine and means "anticipation" in translation. That is, in the full sense of the word "before eating" - before the main meal. The dish is very ancient, but nevertheless there are several variants of it. Forshmak is prepared with boiled potatoes, cheese, carrots. I do not pretend to be the ultimate truth, but I believe that I have a recipe for a classic foreschmak, which I constantly find confirmation on the Internet.

Ingredients

Herring fillet - 400 g
Eggs - 4 pcs.
Onions - 0.5 pcs.
Sour apple - 0.5 pcs.
White bread - 70 g
Butter - 50 g

Step by step recipe

To prepare this wonderful snack, you will need the following products: herring fillets, eggs, sour apple, white loaf, onion, butter.

Ingredients for a classic foreschmak

You can take a ready-made herring fillet or cut the herring into fillets, gut it, cut the fillets and remove the bones. Boil the eggs hard-boiled, cool and peel. We pass herring fillets and boiled eggs through a meat grinder.

Herring and egg through a meat grinder.

Wash and peel the apple and onions. You will need one medium apple or half a large one. One medium onion or half large. It is advisable to take an apple that is not very sweet. Grind the onion and apple through a meat grinder. Add to herring and eggs.

Add the apple.

Add soft butter to herring fillets, onions, eggs and apple. Mix thoroughly.

Stir the ingredients for the forshmak.

Soak the white loaf or bun in cold water, squeeze it well and grind it in any way. Add to forshmak. You can grind the loaf immediately with the rest of the ingredients - it doesn't matter.

Minced herring.

Finally mix the forshmak.

If desired, you can slightly forshmak with lemon juice or vinegar, and add vegetable oil.

Serve forshmak to hot potatoes. We eat with bread. Delicious, simple and inexpensive.

Jerusalem Salad

Jerusalem Salad is simple, but very tasty and is perfect for a holiday. Although on weekdays it can replace the second course, because it is very satisfying and high in calories. The salad is prepared in layers. All products are available for it.

Ingredients

Boiled chicken - 300 grams;
Tomatoes - 2 pieces;
Walnuts - 70 grams;
Lettuce leaf - 5 pieces;
Croutons - 100 grams;
Garlic - 3 cloves;
Mayonnaise - 120 grams;
Salt to taste;
Ground black pepper - to taste

Preparation

Take boiled chicken, tomatoes, garlic, walnuts, crackers, mayonnaise, lettuce, salt and ground black pepper.

Put lettuce leaves on a dish or a large plate, which must be washed beforehand. Chop walnuts and put on lettuce leaves.

Cut the boiled chicken meat and spread it on the nuts. Salt and pepper the meat to taste.

Apply a layer of mayonnaise to the meat.

Wash the tomatoes and cut them into small cubes. Put it on a layer of mayonnaise.

Put a layer of small croutons the size of a small cube on the tomatoes. I cooked them myself, but you can buy ready-made ones. Chop the garlic and add to the croutons.

Apply a layer of mayonnaise on the croutons. We put the dish in the cold and let it brew for several hours.

The salad is juicy and delicious.

Falafel

Falafel is a very popular dish in the Middle East. But falafel is especially popular in Israel, where it is revered as a national dish.

Traditional falafel - This appetizer is a ball made of ground chickpeas or beans with a lot of spices. And, of course, the classic falafel recipe involves deep-frying ...

Ingredients

Chickpeas - 1 cup
Green onions - a few feathers
Chopped parsley - a small bunch
Onions - 1 pc.
Baking powder - 1/2 tsp
Ground black pepper - 1/4 tsp
Cumin - 1 tsp
Coriander - 1 tsp
Vegetable oil - for deep frying
Salt - to taste

Preparation

Soak the chickpeas in cold water and leave for 12-13 hours to soak in moisture and restore its "vital" properties.

Grind the chickpeas in a blender. The "lively" chickpeas are not at all like the lifeless "pebbles" that we see when buying. Therefore, it lends itself very easily to the blender knives. By the way, while soaking in chickpeas, the amount of biologically active substances increases, which, of course, affects the properties of the finished falafel.

Chop the green onion.

Chop the parsley.

Finely chop the onion.

Remove most of the chickpeas from the blender and add green onions, onions, and parsley to it, then chop it all for 10 seconds.

Mix the resulting mixture with spices, sesame seeds, salt, baking powder and previously chopped chickpeas.

Use wet hands to mold balls - raw falafel.

Deep-fry the balls for 4-5 minutes. Chickpea falafel ready to eat. You can serve falafel as an independent dish with various sauces or just like that.

Kugel

Kugel is a traditional dish of Jewish cuisine. They are prepared from rice, matzo, noodles, potatoes, beets, with meat, cracklings, cottage cheese. There are also a huge number of sweet kugels with the addition of raisins, apples, jam, etc. Today we will cook a classic potato kugel. The dish is very simple to prepare, similar to a large potato pancake, only not fried, but baked.

Ingredients

Potatoes - 1 kg
Onions - 1 pc.
Garlic - 1 clove
Chicken egg - 3 pcs.
Salt - to taste
Pepper h.m. - to taste
Olive oil - 2 tablespoons

Preparation

For the preparation of the Jewish Potato Kugel, take the food listed. Peel and wash potatoes under running water.

Grate onion on a fine grater, grate potatoes on a coarse grater. Add eggs, salt and pepper.

Mix.

Grease a baking dish with olive oil. Put the potato mass, drizzle a little olive oil on top, this will give a crispy crust. Bake at 180 degrees for 50-60 minutes, depending on the type of potato and the height of the potato casserole.

Put the potato mass in the dish. Serve the Jewish potato kugel with vegetable salad or as a separate dish.

Hraime

Hraime is an incredibly tasty Middle Eastern dish made with white sea fish in a spicy tomato sauce. Hraime is served in different countries in different ways - with challah, pita or flat cakes. The dish is very aromatic, full-bodied, worthy of the attention of the most pampered gourmets.

Ingredients

Tilapia (any white sea fish) - 800 g
Fish broth - 200 g
Large onions - 1 pc.
Large tomatoes - 3-4 pcs.
Bulgarian pepper - 1 pc.
Garlic - 6-7 cloves
Hot pepper (or sauce) - to taste
Sea salt - to taste
Ch.m. - to taste
Smoked paprika - 1 tbsp.
Olive oil - 2-3 tablespoons
Cumin - 1 tsp

Lemon juice - 1 tablespoon
Sugar - 1 tablespoon
Parsley and cilantro - a couple of sprigs

Preparation

For Hraime, take the food from the list. Wash and dry all vegetables.

Cut the onion into half rings, fry in olive oil until golden brown.

Put cumin, garlic, salt and pepper in a mortar.

Prepare the garlic, spices and salt.

Add a couple of drops of oil, grind into a gruel.

Grind spices with oil.

Pepper, remove seeds and stalks, cut into cubes, grate tomatoes, add to the pan, pour in broth or water. Let it boil for about 10 minutes.

Fry the onion with pepper and tomatoes.

Salt and pepper, add lemon juice, sugar, hot pepper or hot sauce, paprika and garlic-cumin gruel. Cook for about 10 minutes..

Cook the sauce.

Put the fish cut into large pieces on top of the sauce, cook for another 10-15 minutes. Pour sauce over the fish from time to time.

Put the fish in the sauce.

Sprinkle the finished fish with chopped herbs.

Serve Hraime with couscous.

Pashtida

Cooking traditional Jewish pashti with potatoes and cabbage (broccoli and cauliflower). It turns out to be delicious, healthy and authentic.

Pashtida is a Jewish national dish, which is a cross between a pie and a casserole. Moreover, there are several options for preparing the dough, and there are a lot of filling options! The basic principle is this: batter - any filling - batter. Often, even the remnants of previous meals are used for the filling, which are naturally edible: meat, sausage, potatoes or other vegetables, etc.
Ingredients

egg- 2 pieces
flour - 3 tbsp. spoons (a little with top)
sour cream - 2-3 tbsp. spoons of
yogurt or kefir - 2-3 tbsp. tablespoons
cottage cheese - 50 g
butter - 25 g
salt - 1 pinch
soda - a little
cauliflower - 3-5inflorescences
broccoli- 3-5 inflorescences
potatoes - 1 piece

garlic - 1 clove
dry aromatic herbs
fresh herbs to taste
hard cheese to taste

Preparation

If the cauliflower and broccoli are fresh, then cook them until half cooked, and I have them frozen, so I just defrosted them in the microwave.

The potatoes can be cooked to your liking: bake, fry ... or alternatively just dice and boil for 3 minutes.

Combine broccoli, cauliflower and potatoes, add chopped garlic, salt to taste and sprinkle with aromatic herbs. I love the aromatic Italian herbs with paprika and pink pepper, I hope Jewish cuisine is okay ... The filling is ready.

To prepare the dough, combine, mix and beat eggs, sour cream, yogurt or kefir, melted butter, cottage cheese, flour, salt, soda, i.e. just put everything together into a homogeneous mass.

Pour half of the thick dough into a greased form and place the filling.

Above is the remaining dough.

Bake the pastida in the oven at 200 degrees until cooked through for 20-30 minutes.

The Jewish pashtida casserole is ready. Serve on the table sprinkled with grated cheese and sauces to your liking.

Mafrum

In fact, this dish is a potato stuffed with minced meat. The potatoes are cut in a special way, filled with minced meat and stewed until tender in a fragrant tomato sauce.
I like this recipe because the dish turns out to be self-sufficient: potatoes with a meat layer - a dish consisting of meat and a side dish.
I don't think it's worth reminding you that there is never enough garlic in Jewish dishes. I cooked this dish with a moderate amount of garlic, although in the original there is much more garlic in both the minced meat and the sauce.

Ingredients

Potatoes - 5 pcs.
Vegetable oil - 2 tablespoons

For minced meat:

Minced beef - 300 g
Onions - 2 pcs.
Garlic - 2 cloves

Salt - to taste
Cinnamon - 1 tsp
Chicken eggs - 1 pc.

For batter:

Chicken egg - 1 pc.
Salt - a pinch
Tomato paste - 1 tsp
Ground black pepper - 10 g
Water - 2 tablespoons
Flour - 2 tablespoons

For the sauce:

Tomatoes in their own juice - 300 ml
Onions - 1 pc.
Garlic - 2 cloves
Cumin - 1 tsp
Salt - to taste
Ground black pepper - to taste

Preparation

Let's prepare all the products and start cooking Mafrum.

First of all, prepare the minced meat, mix all the ingredients and beat the minced meat until smooth.

We cut the potatoes into washers and then make a cut in each washer, but not completely.

Fill the space between the potato slices with minced meat.

Now let's prepare the batter, for this, beat the egg with water, add tomato paste, salt and black pepper.

Pour flour into a separate bowl.

Dip the stuffed potatoes well in batter and then roll them in flour.

In a frying pan, fry the potato slices on both sides in vegetable oil (1 tablespoon) until golden brown. We spread the potatoes in a saucepan, in which we will simmer Mafrum.

In a frying pan in the remaining vegetable oil, fry the onion and garlic, cut into small cubes. Add tomatoes in their own juice and spices. We simmer everything together for 5-7 minutes.

Pour the stuffed potatoes with tomato sauce and simmer over low heat for 35-40 minutes until tender.

Serve the finished mafrum hot.

Cholent

Cholent or hamin is a traditional Jewish food. Or rather a Saturday dish. Jewish law says that nothing can be done on Saturday, including cooking. All food preparation must be completed on Friday before sunset.

Most often, the cholent was not cooked at home, but was taken to the bakery, where it reached readiness on smoldering coals and remained hot by the time of use. And when they returned from the synagogue after prayer, they took them away.

Cholent combines inexpensive foods such as beans, potatoes, onions, and legumes. But it also contains beef, which, when combined with beans, makes you feel fuller. In different regions, different cereals are also added, it can be rice, pearl barley and other cereals.

Ingredients:

Beef - 500 g
Potatoes - 2 pcs.
Onions - 2 pcs.
White beans - 0.5 cups
Dark beans - 0.5 cups
Variegated beans - 0.5 cups
Pearl barley - 0.5 cups
Garlic - 1 head
Vegetable oil - for frying
Flour - 1 tbsp.
Salt - to taste
Pepper - to taste
Paprika - 0.5 tsp.
Ground ginger - a pinch
Bay leaf

Preparation

Soak the beans in advance, preferably overnight. Usually they take 3 types of beans: dark, white and motley.

Cut the meat into rather large pieces.

Pearl barley should also be soaked overnight.

Cut the onion into half rings.

We send the onions to sauté in vegetable oil until slightly golden brown. We put it in a saucepan or cauldron in which we will cook the cholent.

Pour flour into the bag.

We spread the meat, tie the bag and shake it thoroughly. The meat is covered with a thin film of flour.

We send it to fry in a pan.

While the meat is fried, peel the potatoes and cut into 2-3 pieces.

It is better to cook cholent in a cauldron, but we do not have it, so we used a pan with a double bottom. Onions and meat were poured into it.

Pour the beans on the meat. Cut the head of garlic across and send it to the pan.

Pour pearl barley on the beans.

Put the potatoes on the groats, pressing slightly.

Sprinkle with paprika, add bay leaf, black peppercorns, salt, ground black pepper and ground ginger.

Pour water about 2.5 centimeters, bring to a boil. Then we reduce the fire. Cook over low heat, like jellied meat. The dish is not cooked, it melts. Our dish took 4 hours. Usually Jews cooked in ovens for 8 hours. The water, of course, boiled away. Then it was moved to a lower heat. But there is an opinion that you can add boiling water.

Kreplach

I bring to your attention a homemade recipe for making Jewish triangular dumplings with chicken - kreplach. Dumplings are made from unleavened dough on chicken yolks.

According to one of the legends, the triangular shape of Jewish dumplings is a symbol of the three patriarchs of the Jewish people: Abraham, Isaac, Jacob.

Boiled chicken or beef is traditionally used as a filling for kreplach. Minced meat is seasoned with salt and ground pepper without any additional spices.

Ingredients

For the dough:

Wheat flour - 1.5 cups + rolling
Chicken egg yolk - 2 pcs.

Water - 1/2 cup
Salt - 1/3 tsp

For the filling:

Minced chicken (boiled) - 300 g
Chicken egg white - 2 pcs.
Bulb onions - 1 pc.

Salt - to taste
Ground pepper - to taste
Vegetable oil - for frying

Step by step preparation:

Step 1. Dough for dumplings on chicken yolks.

Stir the yolk well with water. Add salt.

Add pre-sifted wheat flour in two steps.

Knead an elastic dough ball. Knead the dough on the crepe for at least 7 minutes, then put it in a bag and chill.

Step 2. Filling for kreplach dumplings.

Prepare the filling. Twist the boiled chicken in a meat grinder. We recommend using chicken breast and chicken legs.

In the minced meat, add the protein remaining from the egg, onions fried in vegetable oil, salt and ground pepper.

Mix everything into a homogeneous filling.

Step 3. Modeling and cooking dumplings.

Spread the dough on a well-floured work surface. Sprinkle the dough with flour too.

Roll into a thin layer. The dough should not stick.

Divide the dough into many squares about 6x6 cm. Place a teaspoon of chicken filling in the center of each piece.

Blind the opposite edges of the squares into triangular dumplings. Connect the sides well.

Boil water or chicken stock. Cook the crepe 5 minutes before fully floating.

Remove with a slotted spoon to remove excess moisture.

Jewish kreplach dumplings are ready. Traditionally it can be served with broth, herbs or sour cream.

Jewish salad with giblets and eggs

Jewish cuisine is very interesting and unique. It adheres to the laws of Kashrut, according to which it is forbidden to combine dairy and meat products in one dish. Therefore, meat salads in Jewish cuisine are never seasoned with sour cream.

Ingredients

Eggs - 2-3 pcs;
Chicken liver - 5 pcs;
Chicken hearts - 10 pcs;
Green onions - a small bunch;
Ground black pepper;
Salt;
Chicken fat - 2 tablespoons

Preparation

Rinse hearts well and boil for 1.5 - 2 hours.

Boil the liver in boiling water for 5-7 minutes.

Let the hearts and liver cool. Boil the eggs hard-boiled for 7-8 minutes. Cool them under cold water. Clean up. Cut into small pieces.

Cut the hearts into strips.

Cut the liver into strips as well.

Wash green onions, dry and chop finely.

Melt the chicken fat. Mix chopped giblets with eggs. Season with pepper and salt to taste. Pour hot chicken fat over the salad and mix well. Garnish the salad with green onions on top.

Serve the salad warm.

Matsebray

Matzebray is literally translated from Yiddish as "fried matzo". Matzah is soaked in water or broth, mixed with an egg and cooked in a little vegetable or butter until golden brown on both sides. Matsebray is often prepared with different fillings. Let's make a matzebray with fried mushrooms. Despite the simplicity of the products, the dish turns out to be very tasty and cooks very quickly.

Ingredients

Matza - 150 g
Chicken egg - 2 pcs.
Bulb onions - 1 pc.
Mushrooms - 4-5 pcs.
Garlic - 1 clove
Dill - a couple of sprigs
Water or broth - 1/3 cup
Sea salt - to taste
Vegetable oil - 4 tbsp.

Preparation

The matzah needs to be chopped up.

Pour in a little water or broth (it should cover the matzo a little, but the matzah should not float in it), salt, pepper, leave to swell for a few minutes.

While the matzah is swelling, finely chop the onion and mushrooms, fry in 2 tablespoons of vegetable oil.

Add chopped garlic and dill, salt and pepper.

Add eggs to matzah, salt and pepper.

Stir the matzah dough.

Preheat a frying pan, pour in 2 tablespoons of vegetable oil, pour half of the matzah dough. Spread the mushroom filling on the dough in an even layer.

Pour out the remaining dough, smooth it out evenly. You need to cook matsebray over low heat until golden brown.

Turn gently so as not to break the matzebray and cook on the other side. If desired, the cake can be turned over several times during cooking.

Serving matsebray hot, but cold it is also delicious.

Esik-fleisch

The delicious and aromatic meat dish of Jewish cuisine can be prepared according to this recipe! Esik-fleish translates as "Sweet and sour meat". Thanks to spices, prunes and sugar, we get sweetness, and rye bread, lemon juice and tomatoes give the dish acidity.

The dish is very tasty, the meat is tender, the sauce is thick, thanks to the long simmering.

Ingredients

Beef - 500 g
Rye bread - 100 g
Onions - 1 pc.
Prunes - 70 g
Butter - 30 g
Vegetable oil - 1 tbsp.
Tomatoes in their own juice - 100 g
Lemon juice - 1 tbsp.
Cinnamon - 1 stick
Bay leaf - 1 pc.
Cumin - 0.5 tsp
Cloves - 2 pcs.

Sugar - 1 tsp
Chili pepper - 1 pc.
Salt to taste

Preparation

Let's prepare all the ingredients according to the list and start preparing the esic-fleisch.

Wash the beef, clean it of films and veins and cut it into rather large pieces.

Heat the butter and vegetable oils in a frying pan and fry the pieces of meat over high heat.

Add diced onion to the meat and fry for another 3-4 minutes.

Cut the prunes into halves and add to the pan. We also put tomatoes in their own juice there.

Add spices: cinnamon, cumin, bay leaf, cloves. Salt the meat.

We also add a little sugar, cut the chili pepper into circles. If you like more spicy dishes, you can put more pepper.

Add lemon juice to the pan.

Cut off the crust from rye bread and cut the bread into cubes. We spread the bread to the meat. It's time to transfer all the ingredients from the frying pan to a cauldron or refractory pan with a double bottom, add water so that it completely covers the meat, try the meat again with salt and salt, if necessary.

Let the meat simmer over low heat for 60 minutes. During this time, the beef will become very soft, aromatic and tender. The bread will dissolve and become a thickener for the sauce, giving it a certain sourness.

Such meat is good to serve on a bread cake or pita bread. I was serving esic-flush on unleavened matzah.

"Gefilte fish"

Gefilte fish or stuffed fish is a dish of Jewish cuisine. It is served as a snack, as well as at lunch, cold or warm. The dish is incredibly tasty, you have to try it to appreciate it.

To prepare it, you need to take the following products: fresh fish (carp, silver carp, white carp, blue bream, pike), egg, white loaf, onion, sunflower oil, carrots, beets, black pepper, salt and sugar.

Ingredients

Silver carcass - 1 kg;
Onions - 2 pieces;
White loaf - 100 grams;
Sunflower oil - 30 milliliters;
Carrots - 1 piece;
Beets - 1 piece;
Egg - 1 piece;
Salt to taste;
Sugar to taste;
Ground black pepper - to taste;
Bay leaf

Preparation

Separate the fish fillet from the ridge and cut the fillet. This fish is very meaty. We do not discard the remaining skin and the ridge of the fish.

Grind the silver carp fillet twice through a meat grinder. And also one onion and a loaf soaked in cold water.

We add the egg, salt and pepper to taste. Actually, the dish should be quite spicy, but you don't need to put in a lot of pepper anyway.

Mix the minced meat very thoroughly, gradually adding 100 milliliters of water for splendor and sunflower oil.

The bottom of the non-stick pan is lined with fish ridge, husks of two onions, carrot and beetroot sliced into circles.

We wet our hands in water and form oblong cutlets. Cut the remaining skin of the fish into ribbons and wrap the cutlets in them. It won't be enough for all the cutlets, but it doesn't matter.

Pour water carefully along the side of the pan so as not to wash out the cutlets. The water should cover the cutlets completely. We put the bay leaf. We put the pan with fish on fire, bring to a boil and reduce the heat to a minimum. The fish should languish, not boil. You can cook without a lid, I cover, but not completely. After an hour of cooking, add salt, ground black pepper and sugar to taste. We try the broth and if you are missing something, add it. Add some water. Cook for another hour.

The gefilte fish will be ready in two hours.

We spread the cutlets in a dish and fill with strained broth.

We put the dish in the cold. The broth will harden and the fish will be in jelly

Shakshuka with spinach and basil

Classic shakshuka is prepared with tomatoes or with tomato sauce. This Israeli dish is very popular both among the guests of the country and among the locals. The proposed option is a little supplemented, that is, spinach and basil will also be added to the base of the dish. Such shakshuka turns out to be very aromatic. The regular or alternative variation can be complemented with yoghurt and a crispy fresh baguette.

Ingredients

Chicken eggs - 3 pcs.
Spinach - 30 g
Fresh basil - 10 g
Oil for frying - 1 tbsp.
Canned Tomatoes - 150 g
Salt - to taste
Spices - to taste

Preparation

Prepare all the food you need for the spinach and basil shakshuka. Green leaves should be washed and dried. The rest of the products do not need preliminary preparation and this significantly saves cooking time.

Open the jar of chopped canned tomatoes. Transfer some to a frying pan with heated vegetable oil. Simmer over low heat for a couple of minutes.

Put the prepared herbs in the pan. You can leave the leaves intact.

After another minute, drive the chicken eggs into the pan. To make them stabilize faster from below, make indentations in the tomato layer with a spoon or spatula. Season the eggs with salt and spices.

Fry the shakshuka with spinach and basil until the eggs are cooked to the desired degree - literally another 5-7 minutes. Serve the shakshuka hot, you can directly in a frying pan or on a plate.

Khatsilim

A popular Middle Eastern eggplant snack is Khatsilim. And if you have not tried this culinary masterpiece yet, now is the time to cook it, especially since it is very easy to do. We are sure that khatsilim - baked eggplant with spices and mayonnaise, will take its rightful place among favorite snacks.

Ingredients

eggplant- 1 kg.
mayonnaise - 2 tablespoons
lemon juice - 1 tablespoon
sugar - 2 tsp
garlic - 1 clove
salt - 1/2 tsp
ground black pepper - ½ tsp.
olive oil - 1 tablespoon

Step-by-step recipe for cooking

1. Heat the oven to 200 ° C and bake the eggplants for 40 minutes, pierce the eggplants with a fork in several places.

2. Cut the eggplant in half and use a spoon to remove the eggplant pulp.

3. Chop the eggplant with a knife.

4. Put chopped eggplants in a bowl and add garlic, lemon juice, salt, pepper, mayonnaise and mix to a homogeneous consistency.

Hummus

Ingredients

chickpeas - 350 gr.
sesame seeds - 80 gr.
olive oil - 100 ml.
garlic - 3 cloves
salt
pepper, spices
juice 1/2 lemon

Step by step recipe

Soak chickpeas for 8-10 hours in cold water.

Cook for 2 hours over moderate heat.

Drain off the water so that the chickpeas are lightly covered with water.

Punch with a hand blender.

Fry sesame seeds in a dry frying pan.

Cool, grind.

Add chopped garlic and oil to the ground sesame seeds and make a thin paste.

Add sesame paste to the chickpeas, add salt, spices, pepper, lemon juice and beat again with a blender until smooth.

Serve with olive oil.

Khoyagusht

Ingredients

homemade chicken - 1200 g
onions (heads of the same size so that they cook evenly) - 1 kg
chestnuts - 300 g
chicken eggs - 5 pcs.
vegetable oil for frying - 50-70 g
salt
pepper ground black
pepper ground red
turmeric - ½ tsp.

Step-by-step recipe for cooking

In a deep saucepan with a wide bottom, put the chicken carcass, around it place the peeled onions, cut in half with a knife to make it easier to boil.

Fill with water, barely covering the carcass. Simmer over medium heat until cooked through. The chicken's meat should move away from the bones by itself, and the onion should be completely cooked until the head is transparent.

While the chicken is being cooked, tackle the chestnuts. Boil them until tender, cool and peel.

Remove the chicken and onion from the broth, cool slightly.

Turn boiled onion into mashed potatoes and send to a frying pan with vegetable oil.

In the meantime, disassemble the chicken meat into feathers, small enough. Send it to the bow. Stir, simmer. Add chestnuts. Simmer again for a while. Then salt and pepper to taste, add turmeric. If the mass is dry, pour part of the remaining broth into it and bring to the desired consistency. The finished dish should not be dry.

Beat raw eggs into a bowl, beat them with a whisk, and season with salt.

Then pour eggs evenly over the top of the pan.

Now you need to let the egg crust set and harden completely. This can be done under a closed lid in a frying pan. Some are baked in the oven.

Ready Khoyagusht is cut into portions and is traditionally served with Osh - boiled rice, pilaf.

Majadra with red lentils

Lentils Majadra is a very popular Jewish dish in Israel.

A side dish of rice and lentils seasoned with fried onions is sometimes jokingly referred to as Esau's favorite dish (from the biblical story of lentil stew).

Due to its high protein content, Majadra is a hearty, tasty dish.

Majadra is served as a side dish for meat or fish, or as an independent vegetarian dish.

Ingredients

parboiled basmati rice "mistral" - 50 gr.
red lentils "mistral" - 20 gr.
onions - 2 pcs.
olive oil - 3 tablespoons
hot water - 1 1/2 tbsp.
turmeric
salt pepper
greens

Step by step recipe

1. Cut the onion into half rings.

2. Fry the onion in hot oil until brown.

3. Then add rice to the onion, add hot water.

4. Season with salt, pepper, add turmeric to taste.

5. Cover and cook over low heat for 7 minutes.

6. Then add lentils and cook for another 15 minutes.

7. When serving, garnish with herbs.

Bakhsh in a bag

Ingredients

mutton - 350 g
mutton fat tail - 150 g
beef liver - 250 g
long-grain rice - 500 g
onion-1 piece
salt
pepper -2 tsp.
olive oil
cilantro - 2-3
bunches fresh basil - 1 bunch

Step-by-step cooking recipe

1. Pour rice with warm water, salt and leave in water for an hour.

2. Cut the liver into medium pieces and blanch for a couple of minutes in hot oil.

3. Then cut the liver small cubes.

4. Then also finely chop the meat and fat tail.

5. Cut the onion into rings.

6. Chop the greens also finely.

7. Then in a bowl, mix all the ingredients with rice, salt, pepper (at least 2 teaspoons of ground black pepper) and pour with olive oil.

8. We take a bag for cooking (I made it from a kitchen towel) and put pilaf in it. The most important thing is the correct bagging. If the bag is tied very tightly and stuffed tightly with pilaf, the rice will have nowhere to grow and there is a risk that the pilaf will be damp, but if, on the contrary, the bag is loosely tied and put in little pilaf, then the rice will boil down very quickly and you will get porridge. There will be about 10% of free space, in this case pilaf will turn out to be what you need.

9. Next, cook Bakhsh in a bag in boiling water for 2.5 hours. First, 1.15 hours on one side and 1.15 hours on the other.

10. Serve decorated with greens.

You can decorate with parsley.

Carrot pie with almonds

Ingredients

flour (for sprinkling the pan),
4 eggs (separate the yolks from the whites),
1/2 cup brown sugar,
250 g finely grated carrots,
1 tsp vanillin (optional),
1/4 tsp. tablespoons of salt,
1/2 cup sugar,
1 cup grated roasted almonds,
3 tbsp. tablespoons of flour,
1/2 teaspoon of cinnamon.

Preparation

Preheat the oven to 180 ° C. Grease a skillet and sprinkle with flour. Beat the yolks and brown sugar with a mixer until slightly thickened. Add carrots and vanillin.

Beat egg whites with salt until thickened. Gradually add sugar and beat until thick but not firm. Sweep carefully with the yolk mass.

Mix almonds, 3 tbsp. tablespoons of flour and cinnamon, gradually combine with the egg mass. Place in a prepared skillet. Bake for about an hour. Readiness can be checked by sticking a knife (probe) into the dough. If the dough doesn't stick to it, then the cake is ready.

Immediately after baking, draw a knife around the circumference of the cake to release the edges from the mold. Cool the pie in a pan and remove from the pan just before serving.

Kodafa in syrup

In Jerusalem and throughout the Middle East, kodafu are made on the huge metal trays. They can be seen when the vendors carry them by placing the tray on their head. This sweet treat is usually made with kadaif, a lump of sweet dough that can be bought ready-made. This version uses couscous, which gives an excellent and irresistible result.

Ingredients

200-250 g couscous
500 ml boiling water
130-200 g butter, diced into small cubes
1 egg
A pinch of salt
400 g ricotta cheese
175 g cheese, such as mozzarella, taleggio or monterey jack, grated or finely chopped
350 ml of liquid clear honey
2-3 pinches of saffron or ground cinnamon
120 ml of water

1 tsp of orange water or lemon juice
6 tablespoons of chopped pistachios

Preparation

1. Put couscous in a large bowl and pour boiling water over. Stir with a fork and leave for 30 minutes until the water is absorbed.

2. When the couscous is cool enough to handle with your hands, break all the lumps with your hands.

3. Add the butter to the couscous, then stir in the beaten egg and salt.

4. Preheat the oven to 200 grams C. Spread the couscous into a round shape with a diameter of 25-30 cm.

5. In a bowl, mix the ricotta and other cheese and add 2 tablespoons of honey. Distribute over the couscous and cover with the remaining couscous. Press lightly and bake for 10-15 minutes.

6. Meanwhile, put the remaining honey, saffron or cinnamon and water in a saucepan. Bring to a boil, then simmer for 5-7 minutes, until the liquid turns into syrup. Remove from heat and add orange water or lemon juice.

7. When the kodafa is ready, place under the grill and cook until a brown crust appears on top.

8. Sprinkle pistachios on top. Serve warm, cut into slices, drizzle with syrup.

www.ingramcontent.com/pod-product-compliance
Ingram Content Group UK Ltd.
Pitfield, Milton Keynes, MK11 3LW, UK
UKHW061828190726
13853UKWH00009B/2505